Creative Nail Art

for the Crafty *Fashionista*

by Mary Meinking

FashionCraft
Studio

CAPSTONE PRESS
a capstone imprint

Snap Books are published by Capstone Press,
1710 Roe Crest Drive, North Mankato, Minnesota 56003.
www.capstonepub.com

Books published by Capstone Press are manufactured with paper
containing at least 10 percent post-consumer waste.

Library of Congress Cataloging-in-Publication Data
Meinking, Mary.
  Creative nail art for the crafty fashionista / by Mary Meinking.
      p. cm. — (Snap books. Fashion craft studio)
  Summary: "Step-by-step instructions for crafts for fingernail art"—Provided by publisher.
  ISBN 978-1-4296-6552-0 (library binding)
  1. Nail art (Manicuring)—Juvenile literature. I. Title.
  RL94.M45 2012
  646.7'27—dc22   2011002464

Editor: Mari Bolte
Designer: Heidi Thompson
Photo Stylist: Sarah Schuette
Project Production: Marcy Morin
Production Specialist: Laura Manthe

Photo Credits:
all photos by Capstone Studio/Karon Dubke

Printed in the United States of America in North Mankato, Minnesota.
122011   006506R

Table of **C O N T E N T S**

Fancy Fingertips

Nails are more than just protection for your fingers and toes. They're also a blank canvas just waiting to become a work of art. With a few swipes of polish, you can make them a main feature or turn them into an awesome accessory. Paint them to match your favorite outfit. Make them shine for a special occasion. Use them to make a statement. The easy designs in this book will please even the most picky pinkies!

The directions in this book are only ideas. You might not have the same colors or decorations as shown. Don't let that stop your style! Let your inner designer create one-of-a-kind nail designs your friends will envy!

Pamper Before you Polish

It's important to prep your nails if you want your art to last. Remove any old nail polish. Then trim and file away any rough nail edges. Soak your hands in warm, soapy water. Scrub under your nails with a soft brush. Dry your hands well. Then finish your prep work with a coat of clear nail polish. Grab your nail polishes, and use your imagination to create the most artistic nails you've ever seen!

Here are some helpful tips to follow while you're decorating your nails:

- Protect your work surface with newspapers or paper towels.
- Use nail polish remover to fix any mistakes and to clean brushes in between coats. Be careful. Nail polish remover can ruin wood finishes and stain carpeting and other fabrics.
- Let polish dry completely between coats, unless noted in the instructions.

envy—to want something owned by another

Star-Spangled Nails

Declare your independence by covering your nails with stars and stripes. This easy design will start a stylish spark for the Fourth of July or whenever you're feeling patriotic.

You Will Need:

white nail polish
fine paintbrush or French manicure brush
blue nail polish
red nail polish
small paper plate
toothpick
clear nail polish

Step one:
Coat nails with white polish. Let dry. Repeat.

Step two:
Use the fine brush and blue polish to paint the bottom third of each nail at an angle.

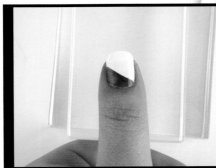

Step three:

Use the fine brush to paint red stripes over the white. Follow the same angle as the blue paint.

Step four:

Pour a small amount of white polish on the plate. Dip the toothpick into the polish. Dab several dots of white polish on the blue. Let nails dry completely.

Step five:

Finish with a coat of clear nail polish.

✳ Variations:

- Paint any country or state flag on your nails. Or paint your nails with your school colors.
- Paint your toenails to match.

patriotic—showing love of and loyalty to one's country

Tiger Claws

Let loose a loud "roar" with these tiger-striped claws. Match your favorite animal print accessories, or wear these nails as a stand-alone statement. Your friends will purr over your feline fingertips!

You Will Need:

yellow nail polish
light brown nail polish
small paper plate
makeup sponge
black nail polish
fine paintbrush or French
    manicure brush
clear nail polish

Step one:
Coat nails with yellow polish. Let dry. Repeat.

Step two:

Pour a small amount of brown polish onto plate. Dab the edge of the sponge in the polish.

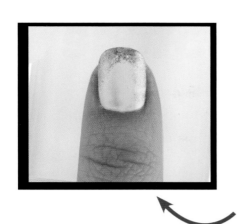

Step three:

Use the sponge to tap the tip and sides of the nails with brown polish.

Step four:

Pour a small amount of black polish on plate. Use the paintbrush to paint black stripes that are widest on the outside of the nail. The stripes should point toward the middle.

Step five:

Alternate stripes, from side to side, up the nails. Let dry.

Step six:

Finish with clear nail polish.

❋ *Variations*:

- Use extreme colors like bright pink and purple instead of yellow and black.
- Use white polish instead of yellow and brown to make zebra-striped nails.

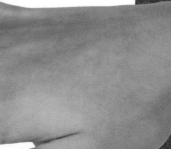

Turned to Stone

Get nails that rock with this marbled design. Add some swirl to your style and accent your favorite outfit. Paint one nail at a time for maximum effect.

You Will Need:

pink nail polish

toothpick

white nail polish

purple nail polish

clear nail polish

Step one:

Paint nail with a thick coat of pink polish. Do not let it dry!

Variation:

- Use any combination of three colors to create marbled nails. Use colors that contrast.

Tips:

- Have your three bottles of polish unscrewed and ready to use.
- Vary the size of the polish dots.
- Swirl the polish on the sides as well as the middle of the nail.
- Don't swirl the wet polish too much, or it will turn muddy.

Step two:

Dip one end of the toothpick into the white polish. Quickly dab three to four dots of white polish randomly over the nail. Repeat right away with purple polish.

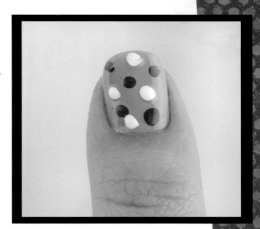

Step three:

Drag a tip of the toothpick through the dots in a figure-eight motion. This motion will create a swirl effect.

Step four:

Let polish dry completely. This will take longer than normal since the polish is thick.

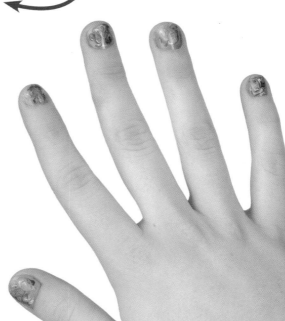

Step five:

Finish with clear nail polish.

contrast—to be very different
from something else

It's a **Jungle** Out There

Tigers aren't the only jungle cat with a sense of style. Show off your creative side with bold colors and a leopard print. Have your colors reflect your mood, and let out your inner animal!

You Will Need:

light turquoise nail polish
dark turquoise nail polish
fine paintbrush or French
manicure brush
black nail polish
clear nail polish

Tip: Vary the size and shape of the spots.

Step one:

Paint nails with the light turquoise polish. Let dry. Repeat.

 ## Step two:

Paint four to six dark turquoise spots per nail. Let dry.

 ## Step three:

Use a fine brush to paint black "C" shapes around the spots. Vary the placement of the Cs on every spot, and don't worry if they're not perfect.

Step four:

Add a couple black dots between spots. Let dry.

 ## Step five:

Finish with clear nail polish.

 *Variation*:

- Use light yellow, light brown, and black polishes to make the spots look realistic.

Nails with Bling

If diamonds are a girl's best friend, then nails covered in rhinestones must be the next best thing. These nails will jazz up an everyday outfit or a sparkly top. They look glamorous for any special occasion. Don't go overboard with the bling—a single jeweled nail should be bright enough to stand alone.

You Will Need:

white nail polish

black nail polish

paintbrush with long bristles

glitter

silver nail polish

6 2-mm clear, flat-backed
   rhinestones (three per hand)

toothpick

clear nail polish

light pink polish

rhinestone—a plastic jewel

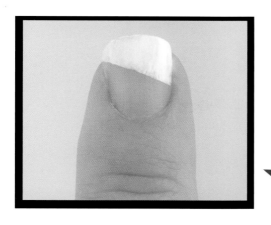

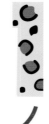 ## Step one:
Paint the top third of one finger at an angle with white polish. Let dry. Repeat.

 ## Step two:
Paint the very tip of your nail with black polish. Do not let polish dry!

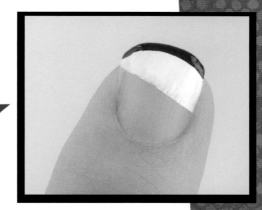

 ## Step three:
Use paintbrush to pat glitter over the wet polish. Let dry.

Tip: You don't need any special glitter for your nails. Regular glitter from the craft store will work just fine.

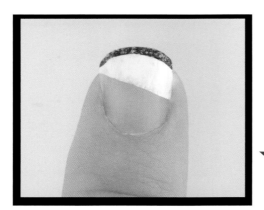

 ## Step four:
Brush off excess glitter from your nails.

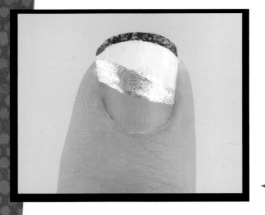

 **Step five:**
Paint a stripe of silver polish below the white area. Let dry. Repeat.

 **Step six:**
Paint clear nail polish over the whole nail. Don't let it dry.

 **Step seven:**
Wet the tip of the toothpick and touch the top of rhinestone. The toothpick will pick up the rhinestone.

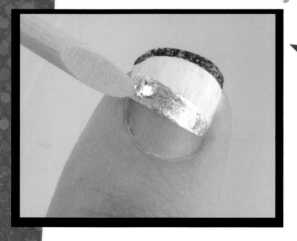

Tip: Nail gems can be bought in small kits and single colors or in containers with hundreds of multicolored rhinestones.

Step eight:
Press rhinestone into the wet polish onto the silver polish. Add two more rhinestones in a line. Let dry.

Tip: Store your nail gems in a clear plastic container with small compartments. That way, you'll be able to keep your gems organized.

 **Step nine:**
Finish with clear nail polish. Paint the rest of your fingers with light pink polish to show off your sparkly design.

 **Variations:**
- Try rhinestones in different colors, shapes, and sizes.
- Use the gems to make letters, numbers, or shapes.
- For a more delicate look, use seed pearl beads instead of gems.

Pretty in Lace

Add some feminine charm to your fingertips with this lacy design. Scalloped lace brings a bit of beauty to any outfit. Wear these nails to dances, social events, or anytime you want to look extra elegant.

You Will Need:

white nail polish
small paper plate
toothpick
silver nail polish
makeup sponge
clear nail polish

Step one:

Use the white polish to paint the bottom half of each finger. The center line should be angled.

Variations:

- For Halloween or a darker look, paint the lace in black.
- Add clear or silver rhinestones for an even more elegant look. (See directions on page 16.)

Step two:

Pour a small amount of white polish onto the plate. Dip toothpick in white polish.

Step three:

Use the toothpick to create a scalloped pattern along the top edge of the polish.

Step four:

Pour a small amount of silver polish on plate. Dab the sponge in the silver polish. Tap silver polish on the very tips of your nails. Let dry.

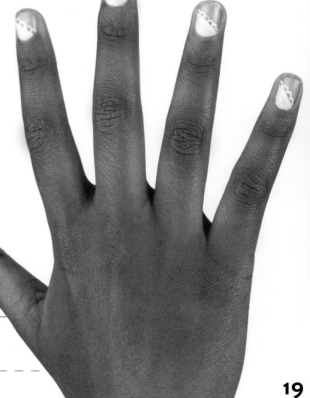

Step five:

Finish with clear nail polish.

feminine—qualities of or belonging to women

Play Ball

You'll score lots of points with these sports-themed nails. Whether you play on the team, cheer from the sidelines, or are just a diehard fan, these nails have team spirit. Show your support both on and off the field!

You Will Need:

blue nail polish
brown nail polish
fine paintbrush or French
 manicure brush
white nail polish
clear nail polish

Step one:

Paint your nails with the blue polish. Let dry. Repeat.

 Variations:

- Move the angle of the white lines on the ball to show the ball spiraling.
- Paint dashed lines on the sides of each ball to show motion.
- Paint your favorite sports ball on your nails. It could be a soccer ball, softball, or volleyball.
- Paint your team **mascot** on one finger.

Step two:

Use the brown polish to paint a football shape on each nail. Vary the location of the shapes on each nail. Let dry.

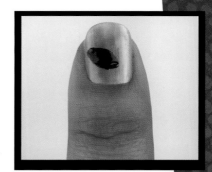

Step three:

Use the fine brush and white polish to paint a line down the football's center.

Step four:

Use the fine brush and white polish to paint the football's laces. Let dry.

Step five:

Finish with clear nail polish.

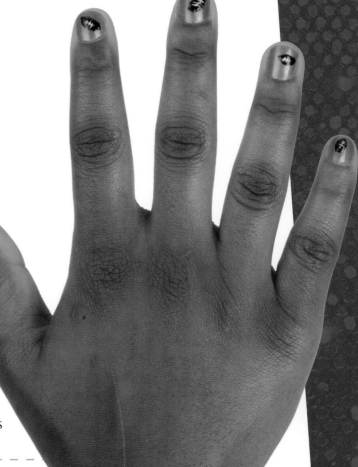

theme—a central idea that is reflected in a decoration

mascot—a person or animal that represents a sports team

Tattooed Nails

Be cool with this tattoo inspired design. Unlike the real thing, these are easy to change at a moment's notice.

You Will Need:

pink nail polish

red nail polish

white nail polish

green nail polish

fine paintbrush or French
   manicure brush

black nail polish

clear nail polish

Step one:
Paint your nails with the pink polish. Let dry. Repeat.

Step two:
Paint a large red heart on your thumb.

 Variation:
- Write "love" or your BFF's name on the banner.

inspire—to give somone the idea to do something

Step three:

Paint a wide white diagonal stripe across the heart. Paint past the heart so it looks like the banner wraps around the heart. Repeat. Let dry.

Step four:

Paint one or two green leaves on each side of the heart. Let dry.

Step five:

Use the fine brush and black polish to outline everything. Let dry.

Step six:

Finish with a clear nail polish.

Sweet Treat

There's no better way to celebrate summer than with watermelon on your plate and on your hands! Paint your smile line to look like a ripe rind. Accent things with simple but sweet seeds. Your fingers will drip with cuteness in this beach-friendly design.

You Will Need:

hot pink nail polish

lime green nail polish

white nail polish

black nail polish

small paper plate

fine paintbrush or French
    manicure brush

toothpick

clear nail polish

 ## Step one:

Paint your nails with the pink polish. Let dry. Repeat.

smile line—the white part of the nail that curves around the tip of your finger

 **Step two:**

Paint the tips of your nails with the green polish. Let dry. Repeat.

 *Variations:*

- Paint watermelons on your toenails to match your fingers.
- Use light orange and tan polishes to paint a cantaloupe or light green and tan for a honeydew.

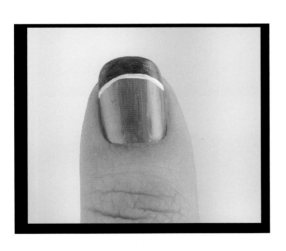

 **Step three:**

Use the fine brush to trace your finger's smile line with the white polish. Let dry. Repeat.

 **Step four:**

Pour a small amount of black polish onto paper plate.

Step five:

Use the paintbrush and black polish to paint teardrop-shaped seeds on the pink polish.

Tip: To paint seeds, dot on black polish and drag toothpick through the dot to make a point.

Step six:

Use the toothpick to dab a touch of white on each seed. Let dry.

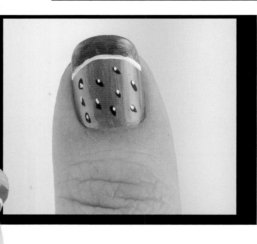

Step seven:

Finish with clear nail polish.

Fly Away

You'll feel like you have wings with these beautiful butterfly nails. The butterfly's colors can match your outfit or your mood. Go sweet with fluttery pastel wings or bold with black lines and dark colors.

You Will Need:

light pink polish
light green nail polish
hot pink nail polish
watercolor paintbrush with long bristles
glitter
black nail polish
small paper plate
fine paintbrush or French manicure brush
clear nail polish

Step one:
Paint your nails with pink polish. Let dry.

Step two:
Use the green polish to paint the top third of your nails Let dry.

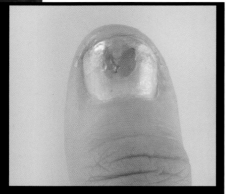

Step three:

Use the pink polish to paint two large, teardrop-shaped wings. The top part of the wing should be larger than the bottom. Do not allow polish to dry!

Step three:

Use the watercolor paintbrush to gently pat glitter onto the wet polish. Gently brush any loose glitter off your nails.

Step five:

Pour a small amount of black polish onto the small plate.

Step six:

Use the fine brush and black polish to paint a butterfly body. End in a point at the bottom.

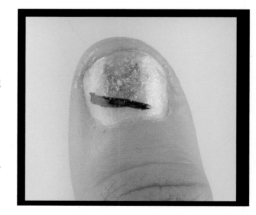

 *Variations*:

- Use orange polish instead of pink to paint a monarch butterfly. Or try white polish to make yourself a moth.
- If you're not into butterflies, try yellow and black polishes for a bumblebee or red and black polishes for a ladybug.

Step seven:
Outline wings in black. Add two thin black antennae.

Step eight:
Use the black polish to add designs and shading to the wings. Let dry.

Step nine:
Finish with clear nail polish.

Tip: If the black outline is too thick, try using a toothpick instead of the fine brush.

Glossary

contrast (kahn-TRAST)—to be very different from something else

envy (EN-vee)—to want something owned by another

feminine (feh-MUH-nin)—qualities of or belonging to women

inspire (in-SPIRE)—to give someone the idea to do something

mascot (MAS-kot)—a person or animal that represents a sports team

patriotic (pay-tree-OT-ik)—showing love of and loyalty to one's country

rhinestone (RINE-stone)—a plastic jewel used in crafts and jewelry making

smile line (SMILE LINE)—the white part of the nail that curves around the tip of your finger

theme (THEEM)—a central idea that is reflected in a decoration

Read **More**

Boonyadhistarn, Thiranut. *Fingernail Art: Dazzling Fingers and Terrific Toes*. Crafts. Mankato, Minn.: Capstone Press, 2007.

Fallingant, Erin. *Spa Fun: Pampering Tips and Treatments for Girls*. Middleton, Wis.: American Girl Pub., 2009.

Maurer, Tracy Nelson. *Fingernail Art*. Creative Crafts for Kids. Vero Beach, Fla.: Rourke Pub. LLC, 2009.

Internet Sites

FactHound offers a safe, fun way to find Internet sites related to this book. All of the sites on FactHound have been researched by our staff.

Here's all you do:

Visit www.facthound.com

Type in this code: 9781429665520

Check out projects, games and lots more at
www.capstonekids.com

Index